whippet

understanding and caring for your breed

Written by
Molly McConkey & Rebecca Phillips-Griffiths

whippet

understanding and
caring for your breed

Written by
Molly McConkey & Rebecca Phillips-Griffiths

Pet Book Publishing Company

The Old Hen House, St Martin's Farm, Zeals, Warminster, Wiltshire,
BA12 6NZ. United Kingdom

Printed by Printworks Global Ltd., London & Hong Kong

ISBN: 978-1-906305-79-6
ISBN: 1-906305-79-X

Acknowledgements

The publishers would like to thank the following for help with
photography: Molly McConkey (Barmill), Rebecca Phillips-Griffiths
(Astri), Pauline Oliver (pages 30-31, 150-151), Catriona Price
(Silkdance), Angela Bayley (Whisterfield), Monique Post, Tracy
Morgan (www.animalphotographer.co.uk) and Mary Turney.

Contents

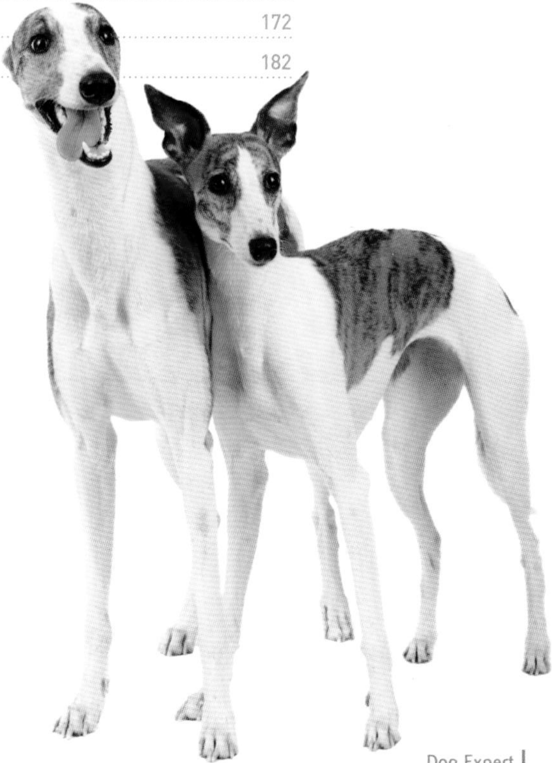

Introducing the Whippet

The Whippet is the ultimate all-purpose dog, combining speed, elegance and intelligence with a loving disposition. Not too big and not to small, he will fit in with a variety of different lifestyles. His only stipulation is that he must be at the centre of family life.

Sighthound breeds

The Whippet is a member of the sighthound family, which is composed of hounds that were specifically bred to hunt by sight. They include the mighty Irish Wolfhound, hunter of wolves and wild elk, the glamorous Afghan Hound, which pursued hares and gazelle, and the Greyhound, the fastest dog in the world.

The Whippet is, in many ways, a down-sized version of the Greyhound, but he has his own very distinct personality and is valued as a companion and as a racing dog in his own right.

Physical characteristics

A graceful dog, the Whippet is, nonetheless, built for speed, with a well balanced body, a deep chest that allows plenty of heart room, and a flexible spine. This allows him to tuck his legs right underneath his body when galloping and then open out to cover the ground at full stretch. The Greyhound may be quicker, but the Whippet is the fastest dog for his weight and can reach speeds of 35 miles per hour (56 kph).

The Whippet has a short, smooth coat, which comes in a stunning variety of colors, patterns and markings. His coat does not offer much protection from the weather and, as a result, most Whippets thoroughly dislike the rain and will retreat indoors rather than risk getting wet. They also feel the cold, and appreciate a jacket to wear in the winter, and a cosy bed to retire to.

Temperament

The Whippet has gentle manners and would rather insinuate his way into your affections rather than mug you, Labrador-style. He is an intelligent dog, but he has to see the point of training. If a task appears pointless or boring, he can be quite stubborn, acting as if it would be demeaning to co-operate with you!

The Whippet has a sensitive side to his nature and will react badly to a harsh tone of voice, let alone rough handling. Ideally, he needs an equally sensitive owner who will tune into the way his mind works and will establish a relationship based on mutual understanding and trust.

Loving and affectionate with his family, the Whippet enjoys the company of children and can be very playful, particularly in his youth. However, he can be reserved with strangers. He is not necessarily worried or suspicious; he prefers to take his time and make an overture if he feels like it, rather than having attention forced upon him.

Remember, the Whippet was bred to hunt and chase, and this instinct remains part of his make up. It may be stronger in some Whippets than in others, but you need to be aware that the prey drive can be such that your dog will become completely deaf to your calls if he is in pursuit of quarry. In this instance, you cannot count it as disobedience; instinct is dictating his behavior.

Whippet owners accept this as an intrinsic aspect of the breed, which needs to be managed. For the most part, this means only allowing a Whippet off lead in places where you are confident that there is no livestock he can chase.

A hunting dog needs confidence and self-reliance, and from this point of view, the Whippet is often misunderstood. He has a tendency to shiver when he is in an exciting environment and many people mistake this for nervousness. This would be completely at odds with a dog that must have the drive and independence to take up the chase. In fact, a Whippet that is shivering is far more likely to be quivering with anticipation!

Split personality

The Whippet is an outdoor sporting dog, bred to be among the elite of canine athletes. When you see a Whippet at full stretch, there is no doubting that he fulfils this role to perfection. However, there is another side to the Whippet.

This is a dog that adores his creature comforts – so much so that he will, quite literally, snuggle under a pile of blankets. He will sleep, or simply rest for hours, when he has found a desirable spot – bathed in sunlight if at all possible – and preferably on the sofa.

This split personality is a charming aspect of the breed, and coupled with his adaptability, makes him an ideal companion dog for many families. He is deservedly the most popular of the sighthound breeds.

Tracing back in time

Sighthounds have a long history, hunting with their human masters, going back thousands of years. Greyhound-type dogs have been found entombed in the pyramids of ancient Egypt, and there are depictions of sighthounds chasing gazelle and even ostriches, dating back to the time of Tutankhamen (1341-1323BC).

Compared to most of the Sighthound breeds – the Greyhound and the Saluki in particular – the Whippet is a relative newcomer, made popular by the colliers of northern England in the 19th century.

However, some canine historians take a different perspective and have traced breed history back to the Saxon era.

Saxon times

During the reign of King Cnut (1016-1035), a law was passed that only high-ranking nobles were permitted to keep Greyhounds and hunt in the Crown-controlled forests. Other people could only keep much smaller dogs, and so it is very likely that a Whippet-size running hound was developed and kept by the 'commoners'. This may have been as a result of breeding from small Greyhounds, which had been rejected by the nobility.

Just before the rise of the Normans across Europe, the Saxon nobleman Harold Godwinson, the Earl of Wessex, had Whippet-size hounds. A hunting trip to France around 1064 by Harold and other Saxon nobles can be clearly seen on the Bayeux Tapestry. The tapestry starts by showing the history of the English Saxons under King Edward the Confessor before the Battle of Hastings. One scene shows Whippet-size dogs being loaded on to ships in Kent for the crossing to France.

Norman times

Henry II (1154-1189) and Queen Eleanor both liked to hunt with hounds. On her marriage, Eleanor brought together all the lands between the Pyrenees in the south of France to the Scottish borders in the north of England. A stained glass window in the town hall in Poitiers, France, shows Eleanor with her small hounds lying at her feet.

Tudor times

It was during the reign of Queen Elizabeth I (1559-1603) the rules of hare coursing were agreed. Elizabeth enjoyed watching Greyhounds work and it is possible that the smaller hounds also coursed. These dogs could also be used on rats and rabbits and were later known as 'snap dogs' for their ability to snap up their prey.

Victorian times

It was common during Victorian times for Whippets to be raced by miners in the north of England. This type of racing was between taped lanes and is known as 'rag racing'. Whippets were released by a slipper on hearing the start, indicated by the firing of a starting pistol. The slippers were allowed to 'throw' their charges down the track to give them additional acceleration at the start of the race.

There were large money prizes on offer and it was reckoned that a lucky owner could win more money at a single meeting than from his annual wage. It was for this reason that the Whippet became known as 'the poor man's racehorse'.

Developing
the breed

The Whippet was originally bred down
from the Greyhound to produce a
smaller hunting dog, but is it likely that
some terrier blood went into the mix to
create the breed as we know it today.

When rag racing was at is height in the late 19th century, there were two types of Whippet; one with a smooth coat one with a slightly longer, rough coat. It is thought that the Bedlington Terrier, the curious lamb-like dog with a curly coat, was interbred with the Whippet, and had a significant influence on its development.

Official recognition

The exhibition of dogs in the show ring became a popular pastime in Victorian times. Many breeds were introduced to the UK or received official recognition by the national governing body, the Kennel Club.

The Whippet was officially recognized in 1891, and the first show classes were held at the South Durham and Yorkshire Show. In 1896 Challenge Certificates were awarded at a Championship Show, and this was followed by the formation of The Whippet Club in 1899, which to this day has the distinction of being the only breed club in Britain to cater for all working Whippet disciplines.

The american Whippet

The USA was one step ahead of Britain and the Whippet received official recognition three years earlier, in 1888. The first Whippet registered by the AKC was a dog called Jack Dempsey, born on September 23rd 1885, bred by P.H. Hoffman of Philadelphia, Pennsylvania.

Whippets were first brought to America by English mill operators in Massachusetts, and this became the centre for Whippet racing in the US, later spreading to Baltimore.

From an early stage, Whippets were used on the larger 'jack rabbits' of the US, and as a result American Whippets have always been bred to be slightly bigger than their English counterparts.

Top honors

The Whippet has had a distinguished history as a show dog and has carried off the top prizes. In 1964 Ch. Courtenay Fleetfoot of Pennyworth won Best in Show at Westminster, America's most prestigious show, and Whippets have won Crufts Best in Show on two occasions – in 1992 with Ch. Pencloe Dutch Gold, and in 2004 with Ch. Cobyco Call The Tune.

What should a Whippet look like?

The elegant, athletic Whippet, with his fine bones and chiseled features, draws admiring glances wherever he goes. Moving with speed and grace, he is a true thoroughbred in miniature. So what makes a Whippet so special?

The aim of breeders is to produce dogs that are sound healthy, typical examples of their chosen breed, in terms of both looks and temperament. To achieve this, they are guided by a Breed Standard, which is a written blueprint describing what the perfect specimen should look like.

In the case of the Whippet, the Breed Standard applies more particularly to dogs exhibited in the show ring rather than those bred for racing. Although

racing dogs must be typical representatives of the breed, speed and mental attitude are more important than some of the finer points of appearance.

Even in show lines, there is no such thing as a 'perfect' dog, but breeders aspire to produce dogs that conform as closely as possible to the picture in words presented by the Breed Standard. In the show ring, judges use the Breed Standard to assess the dogs that come before them, and it is the dog that, in their opinion, comes closest to the ideal, that will win top honours.

This has significance beyond the sport of showing for it is the dogs that win in the ring that will be used for breeding – and the majority of pet Whippets come from this source. The winners of today are passing on their genes to future generations and, hopefully, preserving the breed in its best form.

There are some differences in the wording of the Breed Standard depending on national Kennel Clubs; the American Standard is certainly more descriptive than the English version.

General appearance

The Whippet is a beautifully balanced dog, denoting speed, power and strength without a trace of coarseness. A true sporting hound, he shows an

Points of anatomy

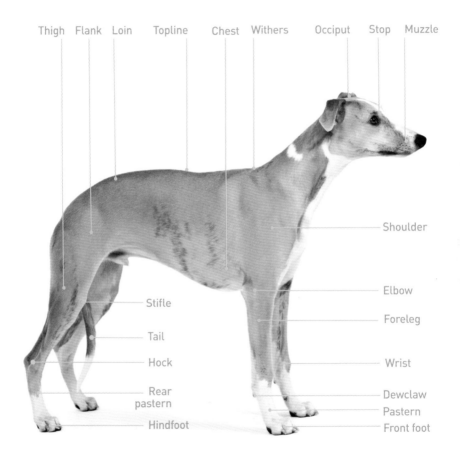

Thigh Flank Loin Topline Chest Withers Occiput Stop Muzzle

Shoulder

Elbow

Stifle

Foreleg

Tail

Hock

Wrist

Rear
pastern

Dewclaw

Pastern

Hindfoot

Front foot

elegance and grace of outline; all exaggeration should be avoided.

Temperament

The Whippet has an impeccable temperament; he is gentle and affectionate and perhaps most of all, he is remarkably even tempered. The American Standard adds the telling fact that he is also capable of showing "great intensity" during sporting pursuits.

Head and skull

The head is long and lean; it is flat on top and tapers to the muzzle, which should appear powerful. The head is at its widest between the eyes, and the stop (the step up between the muzzle and the forehead) is only slight. The jaws are powerful and clean-cut. The pigment of the nose leather varies depending on coat color from black to bluish (in blues), liver (in creams) to butterfly, which is patches of pink (in whites and particolors).

Eyes

The Whippet has oval-shaped eyes – the American Standard asks for large eyes – but what is especially noteworthy is the keen, alert expression which is so typical of the breed. Eye color should match coat color, although there is a preference for dark eyes. The American Standard stipulates that light eyes are

"undesirable", and yellow eyes should be "strictly penalized".

Ears

The delicate, rose-shaped ears of the Whippet are very much a feature of the breed. They are fine in texture, and fold over and backwards; the fold is maintained when the dog is alert, but in repose they are thrown back and folded along the neck. Erect ears are considered a major fault.

Mouth

The Whippet is a hunting jawdog, and despite his fine appearance he should have powerful jaws, which denote a strong bite. His teeth should meet in a scissor bite, meaning the teeth on the upper jaw closely overlapping the teeth on the lower jaw. The lips are fine and should always be black.

Neck

The neck is long and elegantly arched; it is clean-cut with no trace of throatiness, widening gracefully into the top of the shoulder.

Forequarters

The shoulder blades are long, well laid back, with flat muscles. There should be moderate space between the shoulder blades at the highest point of the withers. The upper arm is approximately equal in length to the shoulder; the elbow is placed directly under the withers when viewed in profile. The forearms are straight and the front is not too wide.

Body

In common with all the sighthound breeds, the chest is very deep to allow plenty of room for the heart, which is essential for a dog that chases at high speed. The back is broad, firm and well muscled; it is reasonably long and follows a graceful arch over the loin. There should be a definite tuck up of the underline.

Hindquarters

Although the Whippet gives an impression of grace and elegance, the hindquarters should give the appearance of power. The thighs are broad and muscular; the stifle (the dog's 'knee') is well bent and the hocks (the joint that connects the lower thigh to the lower leg) are well let down and close to the ground.

Feet

The Whippet's feet must be strong and compact; the knuckles should be well arched and the pads should be thick. It is important to consider the Whippet as a running dog and, as such, any tendency towards flat or loose feet, is undesirable.

Tail

The tail is long and tapering and, as a minimum requirement, it should reach to the hock. When a Whippet is moving the tail is carried in a delicate curve, not higher than the back.

Movement

Correct movement is essential for this canine athlete. The Whippet should possess great freedom of action, moving with long, easy strides while

maintaining the topline. The hindquarters are the powerhouse; the hindlegs are tucked well under the body to provide the necessary propulsion and the front legs are thrown forward, but keeping low over the ground. Movement should appear effortless; a Whippet that has a stilted action, which is high stepping, or has short and mincing paces would not be capable of chasing at high speed.

Coat

The coat is simplicity itself – fine, short and close in texture.

Color

The Whippet can be any color, and these can include solid colors, solid colors with white markings, and particolors, which are white dogs with patches of color.

Size

The correct size for a Whippet has long been a source of controversy. The UK Standard, and the Standard for the Federation Cynologique Internationale (FCI), which is the governing body for 86 member countries, both ask for males to be 47 to 51cm (18$\frac{1}{2}$ to 20in) and females 44 to 47cm (17$\frac{1}{2}$ to18$\frac{1}{2}$in).

However the American Standard goes out on a limb with the requirement for a dog that is considerably bigger – males to be 48 to 55cm (19 to 22in) and females 45 to 52cm (18-21in).

Although the majority of Whippets in the British show ring are not at the smaller end of the scale, the danger is that if a dog is substantially bigger he could become coarse, and risk losing the essential quality of the breed.

Summing up

Although the majority of Whippets are pet dogs and will never be exhibited in the show ring, it is important that breeders strive for perfection and try to produce dogs that adhere as closely as possible to the Breed Standard. This ensures that the Whippet remains sound in mind and body, and retains the unique characteristics of this very special breed.

What do you want from your Whippet?

There are hundreds of dog breeds to choose from, so how can you be sure that the Whippet is the right breed for you? Before you take the plunge into Whippet ownership, weigh up the pros and cons so you can be 100 per cent confident that this is the breed that is best suited to your lifestyle.

Companion

The Whippet was bred for a very specific role – to course rabbit and hare at speed – which does not sound the perfect job description for a companion dog. However, the Whippet has proved to be remarkably adaptable and, blessed with his even temper and sweet nature, he is the breed of choice for many pet owners worldwide.

The Whippet will suit owners of all ages, as long as he is given the care he needs. If you have children, you need to make sure that a sense of mutual respect is established early on. Although the Whippet is not a fragile dog, he abhors rough handling and will be very unhappy if he is subjected to it.

If you are getting on in years but still reasonably active, a Whippet will be an affectionate companion, alternating periods of activity with times when he is happy to chill out with you. But you will need to make sure he does have the opportunity to get rid of his energy, even if it means employing a dog walker on a regular basis.

Show dog

Do you have ambitions to exhibit your Whippet in the show ring? This is a specialist sport, which often becomes highly addictive, but you do need the right dog to start with.

If you plan to show your Whippet, you need to track down a show quality puppy, and train him so he will perform in the show ring, and accept the detailed 'hands on' examination that he will be subjected to when he is being judged. This intimate handling is not to the liking of some Whippets, so you will need to work very hard at handling and socializing your Whippet with different people so that he has the confidence to show himself to full advantage.

It is also important to bear in mind that not every puppy with show potential develops into a top-quality specimen, and so you must be prepared to love your Whippet and give him a home for life, even if he doesn't make the grade.

Racing dog

Whippet racing has a devoted and highly enthusiastic following and the breed fulfils its original role as a coursing dog with great distinction, even though he is now chasing an artificial lure.

If you want to get involved in this sport you need to go to a breeder that specialises in producing working stock, and you must also be prepared to put in a lot of work into preparing your dog for competition. A Whippet needs to be fed the correct diet and exercised so that he is at peak fitness in order to perform at his best.

Sports dog

The Whippet may not be the most obvious choice for
the more formal canine sports, such as competitive
obedience, but he is becoming increasingly popular
as an agility dog, where his speed and talent for tight
turns comes into its own.

What does your Whippet want from you?

A dog cannot speak for himself, so we need to view the world from a canine perspective and work out what a Whippet needs in order to live a happy, contented and fulfilling life.

Time and commitment

First of all, a Whippet needs a commitment that you will care for him for the duration of his life – guiding him through his puppyhood, enjoying his adulthood, and being there for him in his later years. If all potential owners were prepared to make this pledge, there would be scarcely any dogs in rescue.

The Whippet is a loving and affectionate dog and he will be miserable if he is forced to spend lengthy periods on his own. If you cannot give your Whippet the time and commitment he deserves, you would be strongly advised to delay owning a dog until your circumstances change.

Practical matters

As already highlighted, the Whippet is pretty adaptable and his needs are modest. He requires exercise, but not as much as the larger breeds, and he is very low maintenance in terms of coat care.

It is important to bear in mind that the Whippet has a thin skin and a fine coat, and he cannot cope with getting very cold or wet. A weatherproof jacket should be considered essential in the winter months.

You also need to give some thought as to where you are going to exercise your Whippet as he cannot be trusted off lead in the vicinity of livestock. This applies to both town and country dwellers, as the Whippet views squirrels and birds as fair game, just as much as rabbits and hares.

Mental stimulation

The Whippet is a clever dog and although he is not interested in monotonous training exercises, he needs mental stimulation to keep his brain occupied. A bored dog quickly becomes destructive, or he may develop other behavioral problems, such as barking continuously, when he is left on his own. He is not being 'naughty' as we understand it; he is simply finding an occupation to fill the empty hours.

As a Whippet owner, you must take responsibility for your dog's mental wellbeing. It does not matter what you do with him – teaching tricks, trips out in the car, or going for new, interesting walks – all are equally appreciated, and will give your Whippet a purpose in life.

You also need to provide a sense of leadership so your Whippet knows you are the decision-maker in the family. If he is left to his own devices, this intelligent hound will run rings round you.

Extra considerations

Now you have decided that a Whippet is the dog of your dreams, you can narrow your choice so you know exactly what you are looking for.

Male or female?

Both sexes in the Whippet are equally affectionate and loyal, and in terms of size, there is not a significant difference between them. The deciding factor is down to you and your circumstances at home.

If there are other dogs in the family, are they male or female, castrated or neutered? This can make a lot of difference to the smooth running of the home. A female will come into season generally after reaching 12 months and then around every six to nine months thereafter.

During her seasons, a bitch may become a little moody and lack patience, but will return to normal after a few weeks. During the three-week period of a season, you will need to keep your bitch away from entire males (males that have not been neutered) to eliminate the risk of an unwanted pregnancy.

Many pet owners opt for neutering, which puts an end to the seasons, and also has many attendant health benefits. The operation, known as spaying, is usually carried out at some point after the first season. The best plan is to seek advice from your vet.

An entire male may not cause many problems, although some do have a stronger tendency to mark, which could include inside the house. However, training will usually put a stop to this. An entire male will also be on the lookout for bitches in season, and this may lead to difficulties, depending on your circumstances.

Neutering (castrating) a male is a relatively simple operation, and there are associated health benefits. Again, you should seek advice from your vet.

Color

The Whippet comes in all colors, and owners tend to have their favourites. In the show ring, brindles, particolors – white dogs with patches of color – and the paler colors (white, cream and fawn) are more numerous, but all colors and markings should be considered equally acceptable by the judge.

More than one?

Whippets are sociable dogs and certainly enjoy each other's company. But it is generally thought that to take two puppies of the same sex from the same litter is inadvisable. They will play happily as puppies and may become inseparable as adults. However, there is a risk that as they grow up and mature, they may question which is the alpha dog.

This can sometimes resolve itself quite amicably, but it could lead to a fight. If this happens, the pair in question may need to be separated and, even worse, you may find it necessary to re-home one of your Whippets for his own sake as well as your own. Obviously, this defeats the purpose of having two dogs in the first place.

In terms of training, you will certainly struggle if you have puppies of similar ages. They will be harder to house train; if there has been an accident in the house, which was not been witnessed, which puppy gets the blame? They are also harder to leash train; if you take two out together they will think it is playtime and while you are correcting one, the other will become confused. They may also become too dependent on each other and if, for some reason, one has to stay at home alone, the other may become very stressed and unsettled.

The best plan is to start with one Whippet so you can give him all your attention and you can learn together. Then, after 12 to 18 months when you feel you have done a good job with your first Whippet, you can consider taking on a second dog as a companion. In this way, the first puppy will be fully trained and will understand his place in the family pack. Hopefully, he will lead by example and the second puppy will follow suit, picking up good habits from the older dog.

An older dog

You may decide to miss out on the puppy phase and take on an older dog instead. Such a dog may be harder to track down, but sometimes a breeder may have a youngster that is not suitable for showing, but is perfect for a family pet. In some cases, a breeder may rehome a female when her breeding career is at an end so she will enjoy the benefits of getting more individual attention.

There are advantages to taking on an older dog, as you know exactly what you are getting. But the upheaval of changing homes can be quite upsetting, so you will need to have plenty of patience during the settling in period.

Rehoming a rescued dog

We are fortunate that the number of Whippets that end up in rescue is relatively small, and when they do it is often through no fault of the dog. The reasons are various, ranging from illness or death of the original owner to family breakdown, changing jobs, or even the arrival of a new baby.

You may find a Whippet in an all-breed rescue centre, but it may be easier to contact a specialist breed club. Virtually all Whippet clubs run rescue schemes and, as these are run by breed experts, you will be given plenty of help and advice.

Try to find out as much as you can about a dog's history so you know exactly what you are taking on. You need to be realistic about what you are capable of achieving so you can be sure you can give the dog in question a permanent home.

Again, you need to give a rescued Whippet the benefit of your time and patience as he settles into his new home, but if all goes well, you will have the reward of knowing that you have given your dog a second chance.

Sourcing a puppy

Your aim is to find a healthy puppy that is typical of the breed, and has been reared with the greatest possible care. Where do you start?

A tried-and-trusted method of finding a puppy is to attend a dog show where your chosen breed is being exhibited. This will give you the opportunity to see lots of different Whippets, and to decide which colors and markings you like best.

At first glance, the Whippets will look very similar, but soon you will get your eye in and notice there are different 'types' on show. They are all purebred Whippets, but breeders produce dogs with a family likeness, and so you can see which type you prefer.

When judging has been completed, talk to the exhibitors and find out more about their dogs. They may not have puppies available, but some will be planning a litter, and you may decide to put your name on a waiting list.

Internet research

The Internet is an excellent resource, but when it comes to finding a puppy, use it with care.

DO go to the website of your national Kennel Club.

Both the American Kennel Club (AKC) and the Kennel Club (KC) have excellent websites, which will give you information about the Whippet as a breed, and what to look for when choosing a puppy. You will also find contact details for specialist breed clubs (see below).

Both sites have lists of puppies available, and you can look out for breeders of merit (AKC) and assured breeders (KC), which indicates that a code of conduct has been adhered to.

DO find details of specialist breed clubs.

On breed club websites you will find lots of useful information that will help you to care for your Whippet. There may be contact details of breeders in your area, or you may need to go through the club secretary. Some websites also have a list of breeders that have puppies available. The advantage of going through a breed club is that members will follow a code of ethics, and this will give you some guarantees regarding breeding stock and health checks.

DON'T look at puppies for sale.

There are legitimate Whippet breeders with their own websites, and they may, occasionally, advertise a litter, although in most cases reputable breeders have waiting lists for their puppies. The danger comes from unscrupulous breeders who produce puppies purely for profit, with no thought for the health of the dogs they breed from and no care given to rearing the litter. Photos of puppies are hard to resist, but never make a decision based purely on an advertisement. You need to find out who the breeder is, and have the opportunity to visit their premises and inspect the litter before making a decision.

Questions, questions, questions

When you find a breeder with puppies available, you will have lots of questions to ask. These should include the following:

- What is your experience with Whippets?

- Do you breed for the show ring, for pet homes or for racing?

- Where have the puppies been reared? Hopefully, they will be in a home environment which gives them the best possible start in life.

- How many are in the litter?

- What colors are available?

- What is the split of males and females?

- How many have already been spoken for?

The breeder will probably be keeping a puppy to show or for breeding, and there may be others on a waiting list.

- Can I see the mother with her puppies?

- What age are the puppies?

- When will they be ready to go to their new homes?

- What happens if I ever need to rehome a puppy I have bought from you?

The breeder should give assurances that they will take the dog back and be responsible for rehoming if necessary.

Bear in mind puppies need to be with their mother and siblings until they are at least eight weeks old, otherwise they miss out on vital learning and communication skills which will have a detrimental effect on them for the rest of their lives.

You should also be prepared to answer a number of searching questions so the breeder can check if you are suitable as a potential owner of one of their precious puppies.

You will be asked some or all of the following questions:

- Have you owned a Whippet before?

- What is your home set up?

- Is your garden securely fenced?

- Do you have children/grandchildren?

- What are their ages?

- Is there somebody at home the majority of the time?

- What is your previous experience with dogs?

- Do you have a dog, or any other pets, at home?

- Do you have access to safe areas where you can exercise a Whippet?

- Do you have plans to show or race your Whippet?

The breeder is not being intrusive; they need to understand the type of home you will be able to provide in order to make the right match. Do not be offended by this, as the breeder is doing it for both the dog's benefit and also for your own.

Be very wary of a breeder who does not ask you questions. He or she may be more interested in making money out of the puppies rather than ensuring that they go to good homes. They may also have taken other short cuts, which could prove disastrous, and very expensive, in terms of vet bills or plain heartache.

Health issues

In common with all purebred dogs, the Whippet suffers from some hereditary problems. Talk to the breeder about the health status of their dogs and find out if there are any issues of concern. Although it is not mandatory, many breeders are now testing for hereditary cataracts.

For information on breed-specific disorders, see page 182.

Puppy watching

Whippet puppies have a charm all of their own; at one moment they are running in wild circuits around you, the next they are sleeping contentedly, usually piled on top of each other, looking as if they would never get up to mischief!

It is very hard to be objective when you go to view a litter, but you must try to put your feelings to one side so that you can make an informed choice. You need to be 100 per cent confident that the breeding stock is healthy, and the puppies have been reared with love and care, before making a commitment to buy.

Viewing a litter

It is a good idea to have mental checklist of what to look out for when you visit a breeder. You want to see:

- A clean, hygienic environment.

- Puppies who are out-going and friendly, and eager to meet you.

- A sweet-natured mother who is ready to show off her pups.

- Puppies that are well covered, but not pot-bellied, which could be an indication of worms.

- Bright eyes, with no sign of soreness or discharge.

- Clean ears that smell fresh.

- No discharge from the nose.

- Clean rear ends – matting could indicate upset tummies

- Lively pups that are keen to play.

It is important that you see the mother with her puppies as this will give you a good idea of the temperament they are likely to inherit. It is also helpful if you can see other close relatives so you can see the type of Whippet the breeder produces.

In most cases, you will not be able to see the father (sire) as most breeders will travel some distance to find a stud dog that is not too close to their own bloodlines and complements their bitch. However, you should be able to see photos of him and be given the chance to examine his pedigree and show record.

Companion puppy

If you are looking for a Whippet as a companion, you should be guided by the breeder who will have spent hours and hours puppy watching, and will know each of the pups as individuals. It is tempting to choose a puppy yourself, but the breeder will take into account your family set up and lifestyle and will help you to pick the most suitable puppy.

Show puppy

If you are buying a puppy with the hope of showing him, make sure you make this clear to the breeder. A lot of planning goes into producing a litter, and although all the puppies will have been reared with equal care, there will be one or two that have show potential.

Ideally, recruit a breed expert to inspect the puppies with you, so you have the benefit of their objective evaluation. The breeder will also be there to help as they will want to ensure that only the best of their stock is exhibited in the show ring.

Look out for a puppy with the following attributes:

- Viewing from above, the head should be flat rather than apple-shaped, and there should be reasonable width between the eyes.

- The muzzle must be strong; a puppy that shows weakness in the lower jaw could develop an overshot mouth (where the upper jaw protrudes beyond the lower jaw), which is incorrect for the breed.

- Ears are difficult to assess at this stage, so look at the parents' ears, which should give you some indication of how they will develop. Bear in mind that ears may go through some funny phases while a puppy is teething.

- The body should be well balanced, neither too long in back and loin, nor too short. The topline should be fairly flat at this stage; if it is too arched over the loin now it will cut away too steeply when the puppy matures.

- The chest should reach to the elbows, and there should be a gentle curve of the underline.

- Feet should be tight and well arched, neither tuning in nor out.

- Bone should be adequate to the size of the pup; it should not look fine or fragile, neither should it be thick and heavy.

- The coat should be soft and fine with supple skin.

- The tail should reach below the hock.

- At eight weeks, male puppies should have a masculine head, and slightly more bone than the females. Check a male pup has two normal testicles descended into the scrotum.

- Movement is very difficult at this age, but if a puppy is constructed correctly, he is likely to move correctly.

It is important to bear in mind that puppies go through many phases as they are developing. A promising puppy may well go through an ugly duckling phase, and all you can do is hope that he blossoms! You also need a puppy with an extrovert, outgoing temperament, likely to enjoy the show ring atmosphere.

However, if your Whippet fails to make the grade in the show ring, he will still be an outstanding companion who will be a much-loved member of your family.

Racing dog

If you have plans to race your Whippet, you should be looking at a litter of puppies that have been specifically bred for this discipline. At six to eight weeks, it is impossible to pick the pup with the most potential; all you can do is check for sound construction and hope they have inherited the winning genes from their parents.

Obviously a desire to chase is essential, which you can test by watching the puppies' reaction to toys being moved along the ground. You are also looking for a bold, confident individual who will stand up to the rigors of racing.

A Whippet-friendly home

It may seem an age before your Whippet puppy is ready to leave the breeder and move to his new home. But you can fill the time by getting your home ready, and buying the equipment you will need. These preparations apply to a new puppy but, in reality, they are the means of creating an environment that is safe and secure for your Whippet throughout his life.

In the home

No home can be 100 per cent puppy proof but a little commonsense and a lot of vigilance are essential for your Whippet's safety, and your peace of mind.

- Decide on the room(s) your puppy is to have access to; this can be changed as puppy gets older and learns not to chew, and is clean in the house.

- Check that all electrical plugs or cables are out of reach.

- For the time being, remove any valuable furniture which the puppy could chew.

- Put away small objects such as coins, marbles, children's toys or anything else that could cause a choking hazard. Children's toys are best kept in a box out of reach.

- Put your rubbish bin out of sight and reach; the smell of meat or fish bones is very tempting, but can be dangerous.

- Keep all medicines and cleaning products out of sight and out of reach, preferably in a cupboard above floor level.

Whippets are very inquisitive, whether young or old. You may find putting a baby gate at the bottom of the stairs will prevent excursions to the bedrooms and attempts at negotiating stairs which could prove to be hazardous.

In the garden

You will also need to inspect the garden and check on the following:

Fencing: Ensure your garden fencing is secure; Whippets can be great diggers as well as high jumpers.

Plants: There are a number of plants that are toxic to dogs. Check this out on the Internet (www.dogbooksonline.co.uk/plants) or by seeking advice from your local garden centre.

Chemicals: Some commonly-used garden chemicals can be a great danger to pets, and must be stored securely. Only use pesticides and weed killers if you are 100 per cent sure they are pet friendly.

Garden equipment: Lawn mowers, strimmers and hedge-trimmers should be used only when your puppy is not in the garden, and should not be left unattended.

Swimming pools/ponds: If you have either of these in your garden, make sure they are securely fenced off. A cover may not be sufficient to prevent an accidental drowning.

You will also need to designate a toileting area for your puppy. This will assist the house training process, and it will also make cleaning up easier. For information on house training, see page?

House rules

Before your puppy comes home, hold a family conference to decide on the house rules. For example, is your Whippet going to be allowed to roam downstairs, or will you keep him in the kitchen unless you can supervise him elsewhere? When he is in the sitting room, is he allowed to come on your lap for a cuddle?

These are personal choices, but if you have allowed your puppy to do something once, he will think that this is 'allowed', regardless of whether you change your mind. You and your family must make decisions – and stick with them – otherwise your puppy will be upset and confused, not understanding what you want of him.

Buying equipment

There are some essential items of equipment you will need for your Whippet. If you choose wisely, much of it will last for many years to come.

Indoor crate

Rearing a puppy is so much easier if you invest in an indoor crate. It provides a safe haven for your puppy at night, when you have to go out during the day, and at other times when you cannot supervise him. A puppy needs a base where he feels safe and secure, and where he can rest undisturbed. An indoor crate provides the perfect den, and many adult dogs continue to use them throughout their lives.

You will also need to consider where you are going to locate the crate. The kitchen is usually the most suitable place as this is the hub of family life. Try to find a snug corner where your puppy can rest when he wants to, but where he can also see what is going on around him, and still be with the family.

Beds and bedding

The crate will need to be lined with bedding and the best type to buy is synthetic fleece. This is warm and cosy, and as moisture soaks through it, your puppy will not have a wet bed when he is tiny and is still unable to go through the night without relieving himself. This type of bedding is machine washable and easy to dry; buy two pieces, so you have one to use while the other piece is in the wash.

If you have purchased a crate, you may not feel the need to buy an extra bed, although many Whippets like to have a bed in the family room so they feel part of household activities. There is an amazing

array of dog-beds to chose from – duvets, bean bags, cushions, baskets, igloos, mini-four posters – so you can take your pick! Before you make a major investment, wait until your puppy has gone through the chewing phase; you will be surprised at how much damage can be inflicted by small teeth.

Puppy playpen

Depending on the space available, you may find a playpen most useful for your puppy when he first arrives home. A playpen consists of wire panels, which can be joined together to make any size; the panels just need to be high enough so your puppy cannot jump out or hurt himself. A cardboard box with a warm blanket for his bed, the floor covered with newspapers, a few toys, and small bowl of water is all that is needed for a safe and secure play area.

Bowls

Your Whippet will need two bowls; one for food, and one for fresh drinking water, which should always be readily available. A stainless steel bowl is a good choice for a food bowl as it is tough and hygienic. Plastic bowls may be chewed, and there is a danger that bacteria can collect in the small cracks that may appear.

You can opt for a second stainless steel bowl for drinking water, or you may prefer a heavier ceramic bowl which will not be knocked over so easily.

Food

The breeder will let you know what your puppy is eating and should provide a full diet sheet to guide you through the first six months of your puppy's feeding regime – how much they are eating per meal, how many meals per day, when to increase the amounts given per meal and when to reduce the meals per day.

The breeder may provide you with some food when you go and collect your puppy, but it is worth making enquiries in advance about the availability of the brand that is recommended.

Collar and leash

A soft collar is best to start with as your puppy will grow through several sizes before he is big enough for a leather Whippet collar. Use a leather or webbing leash with a strong clasp. An extendable leash is ideal if walking in a park or open area, but when walking near a road keep it short so you have control. Your Whippet may see a cat, for example, on the other side of the road and try to give chase.

ID

Your Whippet needs to wear some form of ID when he is out in public places. This can be in the form of a disc, engraved with your contact details, attached to the collar. You may also wish to consider a permanent form of ID. Increasingly breeders are getting puppies micro-chipped before they go to their new homes. A micro-chip is the size of a grain of rice. It is 'injected' under the skin, usually between the shoulder blades, with a special needle. It has some tiny barbs on it, which dig into the tissue around where it lies, so it does not migrate from that spot.

Each chip has its own unique identification number, which can only be read by a special scanner. That ID number is then registered on a national database with your name and details, so that if ever your dog is lost, he can be taken to any vet or rescue centre where he is scanned and then you are contacted.

If your puppy has not been micro-chipped, you can ask your vet to do it.

Toys

Choosing toys is great fun, but do take care because many toys sold in pet stores are not suitable for young Whippet puppies. Avoid toys with squeakers, or ensure these are only allowed when your puppy is being supervised. A puppy can chew through the toy, remove the squeaker and swallow it, with potentially lethal consequences. Soft toys should also be avoided. The best type to buy are cotton tug toys or hard rubber toys, such as kongs, which can be filled with food and provide occupation for your puppy if you have to leave him.

Coat

The thin-skinned Whippet does feel the cold, but there are some lovely coats made specifically for Whippets. By about six months your puppy should have done most of his growing and you can buy him a weather proof/lined coat or one made of soft material – there are lots of colors and designs to choose from.

Grooming gear

A Whippet puppy will not need a great amount of grooming, but it is a good idea to give him a gentle grooming with a soft baby brush.

An adult Whippet will need:

- Natural bristle bush

- Rubber hound glove

- Chamois leather

- Guillotine nail clippers

- Toothbrush (a finger brush is easiest to use) and specially manufactured dog toothpaste.

- Cotton (cotton-wool) pads for cleaning the eyes and ears

- Mild dog shampoo and conditioner.

Finding a vet

Before your puppy arrives home, you should register with a vet. Visit several vets in your local area, or seek recommendations from other pet owners. It is as important to find a good vet as it is to find a good doctor for yourself. You need someone with whom you can build a rapport, and have complete faith in.

When you contact a veterinary practice, find out the following:

- Does the surgery run an appointment system?

- What are the arrangements for emergency, out-of-hours cover?

- Do any of the vets in the practice have experience treating Whippets?

- What facilities are available?

If you are satisfied with what your find, and the staff appear to be helpful and friendly, book an appointment so your puppy can have a health check a couple of days after you collect him.

Settling in

When you first arrive home with your puppy, be careful not to overwhelm him. You and your family are hugely excited, but the puppy is in a completely strange environment with new sounds, smells and sights. This is a daunting experience, even for the boldest of pups.

Some puppies are very confident, wanting to play straightaway and quickly making friends; others need a little longer. Keep a close check on your Whippet's body language and reactions so you can proceed at a pace he is comfortable with.

First, let him explore the garden. He will probably need to relieve himself after the journey home, so take him to the allocated toileting area and when he performs give him plenty of praise.

When you take your puppy indoors, let him investigate again. Show him his crate, and encourage him to go in by throwing in a treat. Let him have a sniff, and allow him to go in and out as he

wants to. Later on, when he is tired, you can put him in the crate while you stay in the room. In this way he will learn to settle and will not think he is being abandoned.

It is a good idea to feed your puppy in his crate, at least to begin with, as this helps to build up a positive association. It will not be long before your Whippet sees his crate as his own special den and will go there as a matter of choice. Some owners place a blanket over the crate, covering the back and sides, so that it is even more cosy and den-like.

Meeting the family

Resist the temptation of inviting friends and neighbors to come and meet the new arrival; your puppy needs to focus on getting to know his new family for the first few days. Try not to swamp your Whippet with too much attention; give him a chance to explore and find his feet. There will be plenty of time for cuddles later on!

If you have children, they may well have been with you when you went to visit the litter, so will have already met your puppy. However, in all the excitement of a puppy arriving in your home, they may act differently so set down some house rules from the start.

Children must realise that puppy is not a toy but something to respect and, at the same time, enjoy as a companion. If the children are quite young but old enough to hold the puppy, make sure they are sitting on the floor. Go to each child in turn; place the puppy on their lap, and show them how to hold him safely. In the initial stages, supervise all interactions.

If the puppy tries to nip or mouth, make sure there is a toy at the ready, so his attention can be diverted to something he is allowed to bite. If you do this consistently, he will learn to inhibit his desire to mouth when he is interacting with people.

Right from the start, impose a rule that the children are not allowed to pick up or carry the puppy. A wriggly puppy can be dropped in an instant, sometimes with disastrous consequences

Involve all family members with the day-to-day care of your puppy; this will enable the bond to develop with the whole family as opposed to just one person. Encourage the children to train and reward the puppy, teaching him to follow their commands without question.

The animal family

Whippets enjoy the company of other dogs, but if you already have a dog make sure you supervise early interactions so relations with the resident animal get off on a good footing.

Your adult dog may be allowed to meet the puppy at the breeder's home, which is ideal as he will not feel threatened if he is away from home. If this is not possible, allow your dog to smell the puppy's bedding (the bedding supplied by the breeder is fine) before they actually meet so he familiarizes himself with the puppy's scent.

The garden is the best place for introducing the puppy, as the adult will regard it as neutral territory. He will probably take a great interest in the puppy and sniff him all over. Most puppies are naturally submissive in this situation, and your pup may lick the other dog's mouth or roll over on to his back. Try not to interfere as this is the natural way that dogs get to know each other.

You will only need to intervene if the older dog is too boisterous, and alarms the puppy. In this case, it is a good idea to put the adult on his lead so you have some measure of control.

Feline freinds

A Whippet will learn to co-exist with a cat, as long as he is trained from puppyhood to understand cats are not for chasing. You will need to work very hard at early interactions and progress step by step, making sure the pair are never left alone together.

It may be easier if the cat is confined in a carrier for the first couple of meetings so your puppy has a chance to make acquaintance in a controlled situation. Keep calling your puppy to you and rewarding him so that he does not focus too intently on the cat.

You can then graduate to holding your puppy while the cat is free, again rewarding him with a treat every time he responds to you and looks away from the cat. When you allow your puppy to go free, make sure the cat has an easy escape route, just in case he tries to chase.

This is an on-going process but all the time your Whippet is learning that he is rewarded for ignoring the cat. In time, the novelty will wear off and the pair will live in harmony.

Feeding

The breeder will generally provide enough food for the first few days so the puppy does not have to cope with a change in diet – and possible digestive upset – along with all the stress of moving home.

Some puppies eat up their food from the first meal onwards; others are more concerned by their new surroundings and are too distracted to eat. Do not worry unduly if your puppy seems disinterested in his food for the first day or so. Give him 10 minutes to eat what he wants and then remove the leftovers and start afresh at the next meal.

Do not make the mistake of trying to tempt his appetite with tasty treats or you will end up with a faddy feeder. This is a mistake that is easily made, and a scenario can develop where the dog holds out, refusing to eat his food, in the hope that something better will be offered.

Obviously if you have any concerns about your puppy in the first few days, seek advice from the breeder.

The first night

Your puppy will have spent the first weeks of his life with his mother or curled up with his siblings. He is then taken from everything he knows as familiar, lavished with attention by his new family – and then comes bed time when he is left all alone. It is little wonder that he feels abandoned.

The best plan is to establish a night-time routine, and then stick to it so that your puppy knows what is expected of him. Take your puppy out into the garden to relieve himself, and then settle him in his crate. Some people leave a low light on for the puppy at night for the first week, others have tried a radio as company, or a ticking clock. A covered hot-water bottle, filled with warm water, can also be a comfort. Like people, puppies are all individuals and what works for one, does not necessarily work for another, so it is a matter of trial and error.

Be very positive when you leave your puppy on his own. Do not linger, or keep returning; this will make the situation more difficult. It is inevitable that he will protest to begin with, but if you stick to your routine, he will accept that he gets left at night – but you always return in the morning.

Rescued dogs

Settling an older, rescued dog in the home is very similar to a puppy in as much as you will need to make the same preparations regarding his homecoming. As with a puppy, an older dog will need you to be consistent, so start as you mean to go on.

There is often an initial honeymoon period when you bring a rescued dog home; he will be on his best behaviour for the first few weeks. It is after this that the true nature of the dog will show, so be prepared for subtle changes in his behavior. It may be advisable to register with a reputable training club, so you can seek advice on any training or behavioral issues at an early stage.

Above all, remember that a rescued dog ceases to be a rescued dog the moment he enters his forever home and should be treated like any other family dog.

House training

This is an aspect of training that most first-time puppy owners dread, but it should not be a problem as long as you are prepared to put in the time and effort. The Whippet is, by nature, a fastidious animal and this will certainly help the process.

Some breeders start the house-training process by providing the litter with paper or training pads so they learn to keep their sleeping quarters clean. This is a step in the right direction, but most pet owners want their puppies to toilet outside.

As discussed earlier, you will have allocated a toileting area in your garden when preparing for your puppy's homecoming. You need to take your puppy to this area every time he needs to relieve himself so he builds up an association and knows why you have brought him out to the garden.

Establish a routine and make sure you take your puppy out at the following times:

- First thing in the morning

- After mealtimes

- On waking from a sleep

- Following a play session

- Last thing at night.

A puppy should be taken out to relieve himself every two hours as an absolute minimum. If you can manage an hourly trip out – so much the better. The more often your puppy gets it right, the quicker he will learn to be clean in the house. It helps if you use a verbal cue, such as "Busy", when your pup is performing and, in time, this will trigger the desired response.

Do not be tempted to put your puppy out on the doorstep in the hope that he will toilet on his own. Most pups simply sit there, waiting to get back inside the house! No matter how bad the weather is, accompany your puppy and give him lots of praise when he performs correctly.

Do not rush back inside as soon as he has finished, or your puppy might start to delay in the hope of prolonging his time outside with you. Praise him, have a quick game – and then you can both return indoors.

When accidents happen

No matter how vigilant you are, there are bound to be accidents. If you witness the accident, take your puppy outside immediately, and give him lots of praise if he finishes his business out there.

If you are not there when he has an accident, do not scold him when you discover what has happened. He will not remember what he has done and will not understand why you are cross with him. Simply clean it up and resolve to be more vigilant next time.

Make sure you use a deodorizer, available in pet stores, when you clean up, otherwise your pup will be drawn to the smell and may be tempted to use the same spot again.

Choosing a diet

There are so many different types of dog food on sale – all claiming to be the best – so how do you know what is likely to suit your Whippet? You need to find a well balanced diet that suits his metabolism and is sufficient for the energy he expends.

When choosing a diet, there are basically three categories to choose from:

Complete

This is probably the most popular diet as it is easy to feed and is specially formulated with all the nutrients your dog needs. This means that you should not add any supplements or you may upset the nutritional balance.

Most complete diets come in different life stages: puppy, adult maintenance and senior, so this means that your Whippet is getting what he needs when he is growing, during adulthood, and as he becomes older. You can even get prescription diets for dogs with particular health issues.

Generally, an adult maintenance diet should contain 21-24 per cent protein and 10-14 per cent fat. Protein levels should be higher in puppy diets, and reduced in veteran diets. If you are racing your Whippet on a regular basis, you may need a diet for active, working dogs, which will contain more fat and protein.

There are many different brands to choose from so it is advisable to seek advice from your puppy's breeder who will have lengthy experience of feeding Whippets.

Canned/pouches

This type of food is usually fed with hard biscuit, and most Whippets find it very appetizing. However, the ingredients – and the nutritional value – do vary significantly between the different brands so you will need to check the label. This type of food often has a high moisture content, so you need to be sure your Whippet is getting all the nutrition he needs.

Homemade

There are some owners who like to prepare meals especially for their dogs – and it is probably much appreciated. The danger is that although the food is tasty, and your Whippet may appreciate the variety, you cannot be sure that it has the correct nutritional balance.

If this is a route you want to go down, you will need to find out the exact ratio of fats, carbohydrates, proteins, minerals and vitamins that are needed, which is quite an undertaking.

The Barf (Biologically Appropriate Raw Food) diet is another, more natural, approach to feeding. Dogs are fed a diet mimicking what they would have eaten in the wild, consisting of raw meat, bone, muscle, fat, and vegetable matter. Whippets seem to do very well on this diet so it may be worth considering. A number of companies now sell the Barf diet in frozen form, which certainly cuts down on the workload, and may suit owners who dislike handling raw meat.

Feeding regime

When your puppy arrives in his new home he will need four meals, evenly spaced throughout the day. You may decide to keep to the diet recommended by your puppy's breeder, and if your pup is thriving there is no need to change. However, if your puppy is not doing well on the food, or you have problems with supply, you will need to make a change.

When switching diets, it is very important to do it gradually, changing over a little at a time, and spreading the transition over a week to 10 days. This will avoid the risk of digestive upset.

The diet you choose should reflect your Whippet's age and lifestyle.

When your puppy is around 12 weeks, you can cut out one of his meals; he may well have started to leave some of his food indicating he is ready to do this. By six months, he can move on to two meals a day – a regime that will suit him for the rest of his life.

Bones and chews

Puppies love to chew, and many adults also enjoy gnawing on a bone. Bones should always be hard and uncooked. Rib bones and poultry bones must be avoided as they can splinter and cause major problems. Dental chews, and some of the manufactured rawhide chews are safe, but they should only be given under supervision.

Ideal weight

In order to help to keep your Whippet in good health it is necessary to monitor his weight. You may think this slim-line canine athlete will never become obese but, unfortunately, this is not the case.

When a Whippet is on the move he expends a great deal of energy, but he is also a natural couch potato, and he does not burn up many calories lying on the sofa!

You need to keep a check on what you are feeding, taking everything into account. For example, if you are using treats for training, remember to reduce the amount you feed at his next meal.

It is very easy to see if a Whippet is putting on weight as he has no coat to mask his expanding waistline. A good guide is to look at your dog from above, and make sure you can see a definite 'waist'. You should be able to feel his ribs, but not see them.

In order to keep a close check on your Whippet's weight, get into the habit of visiting your veterinary surgery on a monthly basis so that you can weigh him. You can keep a record of his weight so you can make adjustments if necessary.

If you are concerned that your Whippet is putting on too much weight – or, equally, if you are worried that he is too thin – consult your vet who will help you to plan a suitable diet.

Caring for your Whippet

The Whippet is a relatively easy breed to care for, particularly when it comes to grooming. However, like all living animals, a Whippet has his own special needs, which you will need to take on board.

Puppy grooming

Your puppy will scarcely need any grooming, but this does not mean that you should completely ignore this aspect of practical care. A puppy needs to get used to being groomed and handled so that he learns to trust you. This means that when you need to attend to him, or if he needs to be examined by a vet, he will be happy to co-operate.

Firstly, teach your puppy to stand on a table. It does not have to be a purpose-built grooming table – just one that is steady and is the right height for you to

groom your Whippet without getting backache. Place a rubber mat on the table so your puppy does not slip and, to start with, let him sit or stand while you stroke him, and praise him for being calm. Reward him with a treat, and that will be sufficient for the first session.

Now try handling your puppy all over so he doesn't have any 'no go' areas. Start by stroking him from his head to the tip of his tail. Lift up each paw in turn, and reward him with a treat when he co-operates. Then roll him over on to his back and tickle his tummy; this is a very vulnerable position for a dog to adopt, so do not force the issue. Be firm but gentle, and give your Whippet lots of praise when he does as you ask.

When your Whippet is happy to be handled in this way, you can introduce a soft bristle brush. Just spend a few minutes grooming the coat, and then reward him. In this way, he will not have to keep still for too long, and, in time, he will learn to relax while he is being groomed.

Adult grooming

This is very straightforward, and if you plan a grooming session once a week that should be sufficient for an adult dog.

Start by using a natural bristle brush and groom the coat thoroughly. The Whippet has a fine skin, so do not be too rough; the aim is remove dirt from the coat.

The next step is to use a hound glove; the best type is one with rubber nodules on the grooming surface. Start at the head and progress down the length of the body, moving to the sides of the body, to the chest and to the hindquarters. Work with firm strokes as you are, in effect, giving your Whippet a massage.

If you want to bring out the shine in the coat, you can use a chamois leather and smooth the coat all over.

Bathing

The Whippet tends to keep himself clean, and grooming with a bristle brush does much to keep the coat free from dirt and debris. The Whippet is also relatively free from canine odor, so bathing is only needed on a very occasional basis. Bear in mind that if you bath too frequently, it removes the natural oils from the coat.

You will need to use a shampoo specifically for dogs, and a conditioner will give a healthy shine to the coat. It is essential that all traces of shampoo and conditioner are rinsed from the coat as any residue could trigger a skin irritation.

Whippets do feel the cold, so make sure you towel dry after bathing, and then use a hair dryer, on a moderate setting, so there is no moisture left in the coat.

Show presentation

This is remarkably easy. A show dog may, or may not, be bathed a couple of days before a show. All that is required is a thorough groom, followed by a 'polish' using a chamois leather.

Some exhibitors trim the facial hair to give a clean-cut appearance, but this is matter of personal preference

Routine care

In addition to grooming, you will need to carry out routine care.

Eyes

Check the eyes for signs of soreness or discharge. You can use a piece of cotton (cotton-wool) – a separate piece for each eye – and wipe away any debris.

Ears

The ears should be clean and free from odor. You can buy specially manufactured ear wipes, or you

A hound glove removes dirt and dead hair from the coat.

Polish with a chamois leather to bring out the sheen.

For a show dog, tidy the stray hairs on the hindquarters...

...and the tail.

can use a piece of cotton (cotton-wool) to clean them if necessary. Do not probe into the ear canal or you risk doing more harm than good.

Teeth

Dental disease is becoming more prevalent among dogs so teeth cleaning should be seen as an essential part of your care regime. The build up of tartar on the teeth can result in tooth decay, gum infection and bad breath, and if it is allowed to accumulate, you may have no option but to have your dog's teeth cleaned under anaesthetic.

When your Whippet is still a puppy accustom him to teeth cleaning so it becomes a matter of routine. Dog toothpaste comes in a variety of meaty flavours, which your Whippet will like, so you can start by putting some toothpaste on your finger and gently rubbing his teeth. You can then progress to using a finger brush or a toothbrush, whichever you find most convenient.

Remember to reward your Whippet when he co-operates and then he will positively look forward to his teeth-cleaning sessions.

Nails

Nail trimming is a task dreaded by many owners – and many dogs – but, again, if you start early on,

Take care not to probe too deeply when cleaning the ears.

Use a long-handled toothbrush or a finger brush for teeth cleaning.

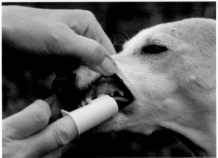

Nails need trimming on a routine basis.

your Whippet will get used to the procedure.

If your dog has white nails, you will be able to see the quick (the vein that runs through the nail), which you must avoid at all costs. If you cut the quick it will bleed profusely and cause considerable discomfort. Obviously, the task is much harder in dark nails as you cannot see the quick. The best policy is to trim little and often so the nails don't grow too long, and you do not risk cutting too much and catching the quick.

If you are worried about trimming your Whippet's nails, go to your vet so you can see it done properly. If you are still concerned, you can always use the services of a professional groomer.

Bald patches

The Whippet has a tendency to develop bald patches on his elbows which can become calloused. A good tip is to apply aloe vera to these areas. It is very good for the skin and also promotes hair growth.

Exercise

While your Whippet is still a puppy, he will get as much exercise as he needs playing in the garden, although it is important that he has regular outings for socialization purposes (see page 123). Road walking is good, as it keeps the pads hard and the nails in trim. However, this form of exercise it is very tiring for a youngster so restrict it to short sessions – perhaps 10 minutes at a time – while your Whippet is growing.

As already highlighted, the Whippet has a strong prey drive, and this means that free-running exercise must only be allowed in a secure environment, such as an enclosed field, a beach, or a park where there is no danger of passing traffic. Remember, a Whippet will chase in a split second – he only has to see a squirrel and he will be after it! You, therefore, need to protect your dog from his natural instincts, and only allow him off lead when you know he will be safe.

Having said that, a Whippet loves to run. It is awesome to watch your dog twisting and turning, and then opening out and covering the

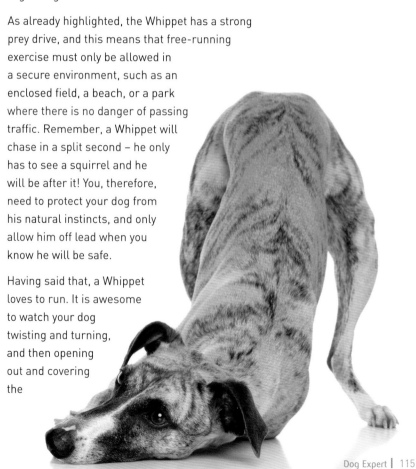

ground at full stretch, so it is worth making the effort to find a Whippet-friendly exercise area.

Obviously there will be times when you need to restrict your Whippet, and on these occasions, an extending lead is very useful as it will give your dog a degree of freedom. He will still get the opportunity to use his nose and investigate new sights and smells, even if you cannot allow him off lead.

The older Whippet

We are fortunate in the fact that the Whippet has a good life expectancy, and you will not notice any significant changes in your dog until he reaches double figures, or maybe even later.

The older Whippet will sleep more, and he may be reluctant to go for longer walks – particularly if it is raining or cold. He may show signs of stiffness when he gets up from his bed, but these generally ease when he starts moving. Some older Whippets may have impaired vision, and some may become a little deaf, but as long as their senses do not deteriorate dramatically, this is something older dogs learn to live with.

If you treat your older Whippet with consideration, he will enjoy his later years and suffer the minimum of discomfort. It is advisable to switch him over to a senior diet, and you may need to adjust the quantity, as he will not be burning up the calories as he did when he was younger and more energetic. Make sure his sleeping quarters are warm and free from drafts, and if he gets wet, make sure you dry him thoroughly.

Most important of all, be guided by your Whippet. He will have good days when he feels up to going for a walk, and other days when he would prefer to potter in the garden. If you have a younger dog at home, this may well stimulate your Whippet to take more of an interest in what is going on. But make sure he is not pestered as he needs to rest undisturbed when he is tired.

Letting go

Inevitably there comes a time when your Whippet is not enjoying a good quality of life, and you need to make the painful decision to let him go. We would all wish that our dogs died, painlessly, in their sleep but, unfortunately, this is rarely the case.

However, we can allow our dogs to die with dignity, and to suffer as a little as possible, and this should be our way of saying thank you for the wonderful companionship they have given us.

When you feel the time is drawing close, talk to your vet, who will be able to make an objective assessment of your Whippet's condition and will help you to make the right decision.

This is the hardest thing you will ever have to do as a dog owner, and it is only natural to grieve for your beloved Whippet. But eventually, you will be able to look back on the happy memories of times spent together, and this will bring much comfort. You may, in time, feel that your life is not complete without a Whippet, and you will feel ready to welcome a new puppy into your home.

Social skills

To live in the modern world, without fears and anxieties, a Whippet needs to receive an education in social skills so that he learns to cope calmly and confidently in a wide variety of situations.

Early learning

The breeder will have started a program of socialization by getting the puppies used to all the sights and sounds of a busy household. You need to continue this when your pup arrives in his new home, making sure he is not worried by household equipment, such the vacuum cleaner or the washing machine, and that he gets used to unexpected noises from the radio and television.

As already highlighted, it is important that you handle your puppy on a regular basis so he will accept grooming and other routine care, and will not be worried if he has to be examined by the vet.

To begin with, your puppy needs to get used to all the members of his new family, but then you should give him the opportunity to meet friends and other people who come to the house. The Whippet can be a little aloof with strangers so do not force him to interact. If you allow your Whippet to make his own decisions, he will be ready to accept overtures, and may well decide the 'stranger' has the makings of a best friend!

If you do not have children, make sure your puppy has the chance to meet and play with other people's children, so he learns that humans come in small sizes, too.

The outside world

When your puppy has completed his vaccinations, he is ready to venture into the outside world. Some Whippets make this transition with ease, taking a lively interest in everything that is going on and relishing the opportunity to broaden their horizons. However, other Whippets may not be so bold, so it is important to take things slowly, monitoring your puppy's reactions and progressing at a pace he is comfortable with.

The best plan is to start in a quiet area with light traffic, and only progress to a busier place when your puppy is ready. There is so much to see and hear – people (maybe carrying bags or umbrellas), pushchairs, bicycles, cars, lorries, machinery – so give your puppy a chance to take it all in.

If he does appear worried, do not fall into the trap

of sympathizing with him, or worse still, picking him up. This will only teach your pup that he had a good reason to be worried and, with luck, you will 'rescue' him if he feels scared.

Instead, give a little space so he does not have to confront whatever he is frightened of, and distract him with a few treats. Then encourage him to walk past, using a calm, no-nonsense approach. Your pup will take the lead from you, and will realize there is nothing to fear.

Your pup also needs to continue his education in canine manners, started by his mother and his littermates, as he needs to be able to greet all dogs calmly, giving the signals that say he is friendly and offers no threat. If you have a friend who has a dog of sound temperament, this is an ideal beginning. As your puppy gets older and more established, you can widen his circle of canine acquaintances.

Training classes

A training class will give your Whippet the opportunity to interact with other dogs, and he will also learn to focus on you in a different, distracting environment.

Before you go along with your puppy, it is worth attending a class as an observer to make sure you are happy with what goes on.

If the training class is well run, it is certainly worth attending. Both you and your Whippet will learn useful training exercises; it will increase his social skills, and you will have the chance to talk to lots of like-minded dog enthusiasts.

Training
guidelines

We are fortunate that the Whippet is a highly intelligent dog and is quick to learn. However, he can have a stubborn streak so you need to make sure that training is always rewarding and there is no trace of coercion.

You will be keen to get started, but in your rush to get his training underway, do not neglect the fundamentals, which could make the difference between success and failure.

When you start training, try to observe the following guidelines:

- Choose an area that is free from distractions so your puppy will focus on you. You can progress to a more challenging environment as your pup progresses.

- Do not train your puppy just after he has eaten or when you have returned from exercise. He will either be too full, or too tired, to concentrate.

- Do not train if you are in a bad mood, or if you are short of time – these sessions always end in disaster!

- Make sure you have a reward your Whippet values.

Most work best for high value treats, such as cheese or cooked liver, but some prefer a toy, particularly if you drag it across the floor and make it come alive!

- If you are using treats, make sure they are bite-size, otherwise you will lose momentum when your pup stops to chew on his treat.

- If you are using a toy, only produces it at training sessions so it has special value.

Observe your Whippet closely when you are training so you can see if he understands what you want and is not feeling under pressure.

- Keep your verbal cues simple, and always use the same one for each exercise. For example, when you ask your puppy to go into the Down position, the cue is "Down", not "Lie Down", "Get Down", or anything else... Remember your Whippet does not speak English; he associates the sound of the word with the action.

- If your Whippet is finding an exercise difficult, break it down into small steps so it is easier to understand.

- Do not make your training sessions boring and repetitious; your Whippet will quickly lose interest.

- Do not train for too long, particularly with a young puppy, which has a very short attention span.

- Always end training sessions on a positive note.

- Above all, have fun so both you and your Whippet enjoy spending quality time together.

First lessons

A Whippet puppy will soak up new experiences like a sponge, so training should start from the time your pup arrives in his new home. It is so much easier to teach good habits rather than trying to correct your puppy when he has established an undesirable pattern of behavior.

Wearing a collar

You may, or may not, want your Whippet to wear a collar all the time. But when he goes out in public places he will need to be on a leash, and so he should be used to the feel of a collar around his neck. The best plan is to accustom your pup to wearing a soft collar for a few minutes at a time until he gets used to it.

Fit the collar so that you can get at least two fingers between the collar and his neck. Then have a game to distract his attention. This will work for a few moments; then he will stop, put his back leg up

behind his neck and scratch away at the peculiar itchy thing round his neck, which feels so odd.

Bend down, rotate the collar, pat him on the head and distract him by playing with a toy or giving him a treat. Once he has worn the collar for a few minutes each day, he will soon ignore it and become used to it.

Remember, never leave the collar on the puppy unsupervised, especially when he is outside in the garden, or when he is in his crate as it is could get snagged, causing serious injury.

Walking on the leash

Once your puppy is used to the collar, take him outside into your secure garden where there are no distractions.

Attach the leash and, to begin with, allow him to wander with the leash trailing, making sure it does not become snagged. Then pick up the leash and follow the pup where he wants to go; he needs to get used to the sensation of being attached to you.

The next stage is to get your Whippet to follow you. This can be a tricky stage as some Whippets decide the best option is to perform kangaroo jumps rather than walk in a straight line. However, bribery in the form of tasty treats will work wonders. Show your puppy you have a treat in your hand, and then encourage him to follow you. Walk a few paces, and if he is co-operating, stop and reward him. If he leaps or puts on the brakes, stop, and allow him to re-focus on the treat. When you are sure you have his attention, set off again and reward the moment he is walking with you.

Next introduce some changes of direction so your puppy is walking confidently alongside you. At this stage, introduce a verbal cue "Heel" when your puppy is in the correct position. You can then graduate to walking your puppy outside the home – as long as he has completed his vaccination program – starting in quiet areas and building up to busier environments.

Do not expect too much of your puppy too soon when you are leash walking away from home. He will be distracted by all the new sights and sounds he encounters, so concentrating on leash training will be difficult for him. Give him a chance to look and see, and reward him frequently when he is walking forward confidently on a loose leash.

Come when called

Teaching a reliable recall is invaluable for both you and your Whippet. As already highlighted, you need to be careful where you allow free-running exercise, but there will be opportunities and you want to be confident that when you allow your Whippet off leash, he will come back to you.

The breeder may have started recall training, simply by calling the puppies to "Come" when it is a mealtime, or when moving from one place to another.

You can build on this when your puppy arrives in his new home, calling him to "Come" when he is in a confined space, such as the kitchen. This is a good place to build up a positive association with the verbal cue – particularly if you ask your puppy to "Come" to get his dinner!

The next stage is to transfer the lesson to the garden. Arm yourself with some treats, and wait until your puppy is distracted. Then call him, using a higher-pitched, excited tone of voice. At this stage, a puppy wants to be with you, so capitalize on this and keep practicing the verbal cue, and rewarding your puppy with a treat and lots of praise when he comes to you.

Now you are ready to introduce some distractions. Try calling him when someone else is in the garden, or wait a few minutes until he is investigating a really interesting scent. When he responds, make a really big fuss of him and give him some extra treats so he knows it is worth his while to come to you.

If he is slow to come, run away a few steps and then call again, making yourself sound really exciting. Jump up and down, open your arms wide to welcome him; it doesn't matter how silly you look, he needs to see you as the most fun person in the world.

When you have a reliable recall in the garden, you can venture into the outside world. Do not be too ambitious to begin with; try a recall in a quiet place with the minimum of distractions and only progress to more challenging environments if your Whippet is responding well.

Do not make the mistake of only asking your dog to come at the end of a walk. What is the incentive in coming back to you if all you do is clip on his lead and head for home? Instead, call your dog at random times throughout the walk, giving him a treat and a stroke, and then letting him go free again. In this way, coming to you is always rewarding, and does not signal the end of his free run.

Stationary exercises

The Sit and Down are easy to teach, and mastering these exercises will be rewarding for both you and your Whippet.

Sit

Sitting is not the most comfortable position for a Whippet, so use it when you want your dog to come to a temporary halt rather than expecting him to stay in position for an extended length of time.

The best method is to lure your Whippet into position, and for this you can use a treat, a toy, or his food bowl.

- Hold the reward (a treat or food bowl) above his head. As he looks up, he will lower his hindquarters and go into a sit.

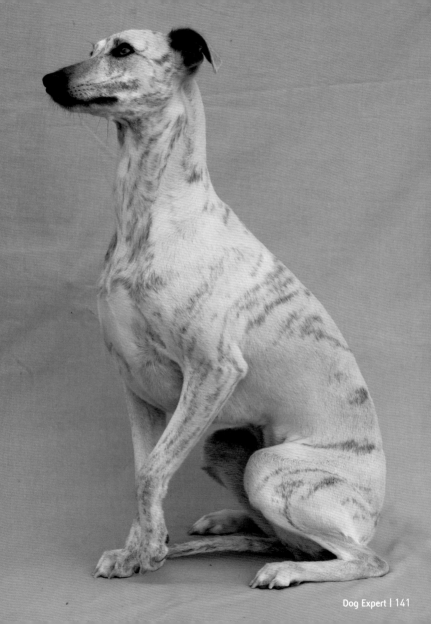

- Practice this a few times and, when your puppy understands what you are asking, introduce the verbal cue "Sit".

When your Whippet understands the exercise, he will respond to the verbal cue alone, and you will not need to reward him every time he sits. However, it is a good idea to give him a treat on a random basis when he co-operates, to keep him guessing!

Down

This is an important lesson, and can be a lifesaver if an emergency arises and you need to bring your Whippet to an instant halt. The Down position comes more naturally to the Whippet than a Sit, so this will be the position he will adopt when you want him to stay in position for longer periods.

You can start with your dog in a Sit or a Stand for this exercise. Stand or kneel in front of him and show him you have a treat in your hand. Hold the treat just in front of his nose and slowly lower it towards the ground, between his front legs.

As your Whippet follows the treat he will go down on his front legs and, in a few moments, his hindquarters will follow. Close your hand over the treat so he doesn't cheat and get the treat before he is in the correct position. As soon as he is in the

Down, give him the treat and lots of praise.

Keep practicing, and when your Whippet
understands what you want, introduce the verbal cue
"Down".

Control
exercises

These exercises are not the most exciting but they are useful in a variety of different situations. They also teach your Whippet that you are someone to be respected, and if he co-operates, he is always rewarded for making the right decision.

Wait

This exercise teaches your Whippet to "Wait" in position until you give the next command; it differs from the Stay exercise, where he must stay where you have left him for a more prolonged period. The most useful application of "Wait" is when you are getting your dog out of the car and you need him to stay in position until you clip on his leash.

Start with your puppy on the leash to give you a greater chance of success. Ask him to "Sit", and stand in front him. Step back one pace, holding your hand, palm flat, facing him. Wait a second and then come back to stand in front of him again. You can then reward him and release him with a word, such as "OK".

Practice this a few times, waiting a little longer before you reward him, and then introduce the verbal cue "Wait".

You can reinforce the lesson by using it in different situations, such as asking your Whippet to "Wait" before you put his food bowl down.

Stay

You need to differentiate this exercise from the Wait by using a different hand signal and a different verbal cue.

Start with your Whippet in the Down, as he is most likely to be secure in this position. Stand by his side and then step forwards, with your hand held back, palm facing the dog.

Step back, release him, and then reward him. Practice until your Whippet understands the exercise and then introduce the verbal cue "Stay".

Gradually increase the distance you can leave your puppy, and increase the challenge by walking around him – and even stepping over him – so that he learns he must "Stay" until you release him.

Leave

A response to this verbal cue means that your Whippet will learn to give up a toy on request, and it follows that he will give up anything when he is asked, which is very useful if he has hold of a forbidden object. You can also use it if you catch him red-handed raiding the bin, or digging up a prized plant in the garden.

The Whippet is not often possessive over his toys, but some think that running off in the opposite direction – toy in mouth – is a great game. It is therefore important to teach your puppy that if he gives up something, he will get a reward, which may be even better than the thing he has already!

- The "Leave" command can be taught quite easily when you are first playing with your puppy. As you gently take a toy from his mouth, introduce the verbal cue, "Leave", and then praise him.

- If he is reluctant, swap the toy for another toy or a treat. This will usually do the trick.

- Do not try to pull the toy from his mouth if he refuses to give it up, as this will only make him keener to hang on to it. Let the toy go 'dead' in your hand, and then swap it for a new, exciting, toy, so this becomes the better option.

- Remember to make a big fuss of your Whippet when he co-operates. If he is rewarded with verbal praise, plus a game with a toy or a tasty treat, he will learn that "Leave" is always a good option.

Opportunities
for whippets

The Whippet is quick-witted and fast moving, and will relish the opportunity to use his mind and his body.

Good Citizen Scheme

The Kennel Club Good Citizen Scheme was introduced to promote responsible dog ownership, and to teach dogs basic good manners. In the US there is one test; in the UK there are four award levels: Puppy Foundation, Bronze, Silver and Gold.

Exercises within the scheme include:

- Walking on leash

- Road walking

- Control at door/gate.

- Food manners

- Recall

- Stay

- Send to bed

- Emergency stop.

Competitive obedience

This is a sport where you are assessed as a dog and handler, completing a series of exercises including heelwork, recalls, retrieves, stays, sendaways and scent discrimination.

The Whippet is certainly intelligent enough to learn the exercises required, but he will not respond to being drilled. If you fancy having a go at this discipline, keep training sessions brief and rewarding.

Obedience exercises are relatively simple to begin with, involving heelwork, a recall and stays in the lowest class. As you progress through, more exercises are added, and the aids you are allowed to give are reduced.

To achieve top honors in this discipline requires intensive training, as precision and accuracy are of paramount importance.

Rally O

If you do not want to get involved in the rigors of Competitive Obedience, you may find that a sport called Rally O is more to your liking.

This is loosely based on Obedience, and also has a few exercises borrowed from Agility when you get to the highest levels. Handler and dog must complete a course, in the designated order, which has a variety of different exercises numbering from 12 to 20. The course is timed and the team must complete within the time limit that is set, but there are no bonus marks for speed.

The great advantage of Rally O is that it is very relaxed, and anyone can compete; indeed, it has proved very popular for handlers with disabilities, as they are able to work their dogs to a high standard and compete on equal terms with other competitors.

Agility

The Whippet is a highly successful competitor in Agility, as he moves at great speed when motivated. Your challenge is to focus his attention, and make training fun.

Facing page: The athletic Whippet will enjoy the challenge of agility training.

In this sport, the dog completes an obstacle course under the guidance of his owner. You need a good element of control, as the dog competes off the lead.

In competition, each dog completes the course individually and is assessed on both time and accuracy. The dog that completes the course with the fewest faults in the fastest time wins the class. The obstacles include an A-frame, a dog-walk, weaving poles, a seesaw, tunnels, and jumps.

Showing

If you plan to exhibit your Whippet in the show ring, you not only need a top-quality specimen, you need a dog that is born with a sense of showmanship.

In the ring, a Whippet needs to show himself off to advantage – standing in a show pose, moving around the ring and allowing a detailed hands-on examination by the judge. A dog that does not like being handled by the judge, or one that does not walk smartly on the leash, is never going to win top honors, even if he is a top-quality animal.

In order to prepare your Whippet for the busy show atmosphere, you need to work on his socialization, and then take him to ringcraft classes so you both learn what is required in the ring.

Showing at the top level is highly addictive, so watch out, once you start, you will never have a free date in your diary!

Whippet racing

Watching a Whippet in full flight is exhilarating and satisfying for both Whippet and owner. The best place to run your Whippet is with a specialist club, which will have enclosed areas where it is safe for the dogs, away from stock and roads. You can get a lot of enjoyment by joining a racing club and measuring your dog against others in a structured environment.

Club racing is designed to be fun and to accommodate all standards, progressing through classes by weight and distance to open class and championships. These meetings are also a great place to socialize with like-minded people.

Lure coursing

No live game is ever used in this sport; the aim is to stimulate a Whippet's natural instincts for coursing. Lure coursing is well established in many countries, and has a highly enthusiastic following.

The 'lure' (a bunch of plastic bags) is tied to a rope or line that is pulled around on pullies by an electric motor specially designed for this purpose. The course pattern is irregular and somewhat similar to the way a hare might run in an open field.

Two Whippets are released from slips, and each has a different coloured jacket for identification. Judges are situated on a rostrum in the centre of the course. The lure starts its journey with the hounds in hot pursuit. Each is judged on the ability to follow the zig zag of the lure and not to cut corners or interfere with the other hound, for which they are penalized or disqualified. Each dog is marked on performance, enthusiasm, agility and speed, and at the end of the day the dog with the highest mark (out of 100) wins its class.

Health care

We are fortunate that the Whippet
is a healthy dog and, with good
routine care, a well-balanced diet,
and sufficient exercise, most will
experience few health problems.

However, it is your responsibility to put a program of
preventative health care in place – and this should
start from the moment your puppy, or older dog,
arrives in his new home.

Vaccinations

Dogs are subject to a number of contagious
diseases. At one time these were killers,
and resulted in heartbreak for many owners.
Vaccinations have now been developed, and the
occurrence of the major infectious diseases is now
very rare. However, this will only remain the case
if all pet owners follow a strict policy of vaccinating
their dogs.

There are vaccinations available for the following diseases:

Adenovirus: (Canine Adenovirus): This affects the liver; affected dogs have a classic 'blue eye'.

Distemper: A viral disease, which causes chest and gastro-intestinal damage. The brain may also be affected, leading to fits and paralysis.

Parvovirus: Causes severe gastro enteritis, and most commonly affects puppies.

Leptospirosis: This bacterial disease is carried by rats and affects many mammals, including humans. It causes liver and kidney damage.

Rabies: A virus that affects the nervous system and is invariably fatal. The first signs are abnormal behavior, during which the infected dog may bite another animal or a person. Paralysis and death follow. Vaccination is compulsory in most countries. In the UK, dogs traveling overseas must be vaccinated.

Kennel Cough: There are several strains of kennel cough, but they all result in a harsh, dry, cough. This disease is rarely fatal; in fact most dogs make a good recovery within a matter of weeks and show few signs of ill health while they are affected. However, kennel cough is highly infectious among dogs that live together so, for this reason, most boarding kennels will insist that your dog is protected by the vaccine, which is given as nose drops.

Lyme Disease: This is a bacterial disease transmitted by ticks (see page 168). The first signs are limping, but the heart, kidneys and nervous system can also be affected. The ticks that transmit the disease occur in specific regions, such as the north-east states of the USA, some of the southern states, California and the upper Mississippi region. Lyme disease is still rare in the UK so vaccinations are not routinely offered.

Vaccination program

In the USA, the American Animal Hospital Association advises vaccination for core diseases, which they list as: distemper, adenovirus, parvovirus and rabies. The requirement for vaccinating for non-core diseases – leptospirosis, lyme disease and kennel cough – should be assessed depending on a dog's individual risk and his likely exposure to the disease.

In the UK, vaccinations are routinely given for distemper, adenovirus, leptospirosis and parvovirus.

In most cases, a puppy will start his vaccinations at around eight weeks of age, with the second part given a fortnight later. However, this does vary depending on the individual policy of veterinary practices, and the incidence of disease in your area.

You should also talk to your vet about whether to give annual booster vaccinations. This depends on an individual dog's levels of immunity, and how long a particular vaccine remains effective.

Parasites

No matter how well you look after your Whippet, you will have to accept that parasites – internal and external – are ever present, and you need to take preventative action.

Internal parasites: As the name suggests, these parasites live inside your dog. Most will find a home in the digestive tract, but there is also a parasite that lives in the heart. If infestation is unchecked, a dog's health will be severely jeopardized, but routine preventative treatment is simple and effective.

External parasites: These parasites live on your dog's body – in his skin and fur, and sometimes in his ears.

Roundworm

This is found in the small intestine, and signs of infestation will be a poor coat, a pot belly, diarrhoea and lethargy. Pregnant mothers should be treated, but it is almost inevitable that parasites will be passed on to the puppies. For this reason, a breeder will start a worming program, which you will need to continue. Ask your vet for advice on treatment, which will need to continue throughout your dog's life.

Tapeworm

Infection occurs when fleas and lice are ingested; the adult worm takes up residence in the small intestine, releasing mobile segments (which contain eggs) that can be seen in a dog's feces as small rice-like grains. The only other obvious sign of infestation is irritation of the anus. Again, routine preventative treatment is required throughout your Whippet's life.

Heartworm

This parasite is transmitted by mosquitoes, and so will only occur where these insects thrive. A warm environment is needed for the parasite to develop, so it is more likely to be present in areas with a warm, humid climate. However, it is found in all parts of the USA, although its prevalence does vary. At present, heartworm is rarely seen in the UK.

Heartworm live in the right side of the heart. Larvae can grow up to 14 inches (35cm) in length. A dog with heartworm is at severe risk from heart failure, so preventative treatment, as advised by your vet, is essential. Dogs living in the USA should have regular blood tests to check for the presence of infection.

Lungworm

Lungworm, or *Angiostrongylus vasorum*, is a parasite that lives in the heart and major blood vessels supplying the lungs. It can cause many problems, such as breathing difficulties, blood-clotting problems, sickness and diarrhoea, seizures, and can even be fatal. The parasite is carried by slugs and snails, and the dog becomes infected when ingesting these, often accidentally, when rummaging through undergrowth. Lungworm is not common, but it is on the increase and a responsible owner should be aware of it. Fortunately, it is easily preventable and even affected dogs usually make a full recovery if treated early enough. Your vet will be able to advise you on the risks in your area and what form of treatment may be required.

Fleas

A dog may carry dog fleas, cat fleas, and even human fleas. The flea stays on the dog only long enough to have a blood meal and to breed, but its presence will result in itching and scratching. If your dog has an allergy to fleas – which is usually a reaction to the flea's saliva – he will scratch himself until he is raw.

Spot-on treatment, which should be administered on a routine basis, is easy to use and highly effective on all types of fleas. You can also treat your dog with a spray or with insecticidal shampoo. Bear in mind that the whole environment your dog lives in will need to be sprayed, and all other pets living in your home will also need to be treated.

How to detect fleas

You may suspect your dog has fleas, but how can you be sure? There are two methods to try.

Run a fine comb through your dog's coat, and see if you can detect the presence of fleas on the skin, or clinging to the comb. Alternatively, sit your dog on white paper and rub his back. This will dislodge feces from the fleas, which will be visible as small brown specks. To double check, shake the specks on to some damp cotton (cotton-wool). Flea feces consists of the dried blood taken from the host, so if the specks turn a lighter shade of red, you know your dog has fleas.

Ticks

These are blood-sucking parasites that are most frequently found in rural areas where sheep or deer are present. The main danger is their ability to pass lyme disease to both dogs and humans. Lyme disease is prevalent in some areas of the USA (see page 163), although it is still rare in the UK. The treatment you give your dog for fleas generally works for ticks, but you should discuss the best product to use with your vet.

How to remove a tick

If you spot a tick on your dog, do not try to pluck it off as you risk leaving the hard mouth parts embedded in his skin. The best way to remove a tick is to use a fine pair of tweezers or you can buy a tick remover. Grasp the tick head firmly and then pull the tick straight out from the skin. If you are using a tick remover, check the instructions, as some recommend a circular twist when pulling. When you have removed the tick, clean the area with mild soap and water.

Ear mites

These parasites live in the outer ear canal. The signs of infestation are a brown, waxy discharge, head shaking and ear scratching. If you suspect your Whippet has ear mites, a visit to the vet will be needed so that medicated eardrops can be prescribed.

Fur mites

These small, white parasites are visible to the naked eye and are often referred to as 'walking dandruff'. They cause a scurfy coat and mild itchiness. However, they are zoonetic – transferable to humans – so prompt treatment with an insecticide prescribed by your vet is essential.

Harvest mites

These are picked up from the undergrowth, and can be seen as a bright orange patch on the webbing between the toes, although this can be found elsewhere on the body, such as on the ear flaps. Treatment is effective with the appropriate insecticide.

Skin mites

There are two types of parasite that burrow into a dog's skin. *Demodex canis* is transferred from a mother to her pups while they are feeding. Treatment is with a topical preparation, and sometimes antibiotics are needed.

The other skin mite is *Sarcoptes scabiei*, which causes intense itching and hair loss. It is highly contagious, so all dogs in a household will need to be treated, which involves repeated bathing with a medicated shampoo.

Common ailments

As with all living animals, dogs can be affected by a variety of ailments. Most can be treated effectively after consulting with your vet, who will prescribe appropriate medication and will advise you on how to care for your dog's needs.

Here are some of the more common problems that could affect your Whippet, with advice on how to deal with them.

Anal glands

These are two small sacs on either side of the anus, which produce a dark-brown secretion that dogs use when they mark their territory. The anal glands should empty every time a dog defecates but if they become blocked or impacted, a dog will experience increasing discomfort. He may nibble at his rear end, or 'scoot' his bottom along the ground to relieve the irritation.

Treatment involves a trip to the vet, who will empty the glands manually. It is important to do this without delay or infection may occur.

Dental problems

Good dental hygiene will do much to minimize gum infection and tooth decay, which is why teeth cleaning should be part of your regular care routine. If tartar accumulates to the extent that you cannot remove it by brushing, the vet will need to intervene. In a situation such as this, an anesthetic will need to be administered so the tartar can be removed manually.

Diarrhoea

There are many reasons why a dog has diarrhoea, but most commonly it is the result of scavenging, a sudden change of diet, or an adverse reaction to a particular type of food.

If your dog is suffering from diarrhoea, the first step is to withdraw food for a day. It is important that he does not dehydrate, so make sure that fresh drinking water is available. However, drinking too much can increase the diarrhoea, which may be accompanied with vomiting, so limit how much he drinks at any one time.

After allowing the stomach to rest, feed a bland diet, such as white fish or chicken with boiled rice, for a few days. In most cases, your dog's motions will return to normal and you can resume normal feeding, although this should be done gradually.

However, if this fails to work and the diarrhoea persists for more than a few days, you should consult you vet. Your dog may have an infection which needs to be treated with antibiotics, or the diarrhoea may indicate some other problem which needs expert diagnosis.

Ear infections

The Whippet has rose-shaped ears which fold over and backwards. This allows air to circulate freely, which minimizes the risk of ear infections.

A healthy ear is clean with no sign of redness or inflammation, and no evidence of a waxy brown discharge or a foul odor. If you see your dog scratching his ear, shaking his head, or holding one ear at an odd angle, you will need to consult your vet.

The most likely causes are ear mites, an infection, or there may a foreign body, such as a grass seed, trapped in the ear.

Depending on the cause, treatment is with medicated ear drops, possibly containing antibiotics. If a foreign body is suspected, the vet will need to carry our further investigations.

Eye problems

The Whippet has oval eyes; they are set in the skull and do not protrude. This is important, as breeds with prominent eyes, such as the Pekingese, are more vulnerable to injury.

If your Whippet's eyes look red and sore, he may be suffering from conjunctivitis. This may, or may not be accompanied with a watery or a crusty discharge. Conjunctivitis can be caused by a bacterial or viral infection, it could be the result of an injury, or it could be an adverse reaction to pollen.

You will need to consult your vet for a correct diagnosis, but in the case of an infection, treatment with medicated eye drops is effective.

Conjunctivitis may also be the first sign of more serious inherited eye problems (see page 185).

In some instances, a dog may suffer from dry, itchy eye, which your dog may further injure through scratching. This condition, known as keratoconjunctivitis sicca, may be inherited.

Foreign bodies

In the home, puppies – and some older dogs – cannot resist chewing anything that looks interesting. The toys you choose for your dog should be suitably robust to withstand damage, but children's toys can be irresistible. Some dogs will chew – and swallow – anything from socks, tights, and any other items from the laundry basket to golf balls and stones from the garden. Obviously, these items are indigestible and could cause an obstruction in your dog's intestine, which is potentially lethal.

The signs to look for are vomiting, and a tucked up posture. The dog will often be restless and will look as though he is in pain.

In this situation, you must get your dog to the vet without delay as surgery will be needed to remove the obstruction.

Heatstroke

The Whippet's head structure is without exaggeration, which means that he has a straightforward respiratory system, and does not suffer breathing problems experienced by flat-nosed breeds, such as the Pug or the French Bulldog.

However, all dogs can overheat on hot days, and this can have disastrous consequences. If the weather is warm make sure your Whippet has access to shady areas, and wait for a cooler part of the day before going for a walk. Be extra careful if you leave your Whippet in the car, as the temperature can rise dramatically, even on a cloudy day. Heatstroke can happen very rapidly, and unless you are able lower your dog's temperature, it can be fatal.

If your Whippet appears to be suffering from heatstroke, lie him flat and work at lowering his temperature by spraying him with cool water and covering him with wet towels. As soon as he has made some recovery, take him to the vet where cold intravenous fluids can be administered.

Lameness/limping

There are a wide variety of reasons why a dog can go lame, from a simple muscle strain, to a fracture, ligament damage, or more complex problems with the joints. If you are concerned about your dog, do not delay in seeking help.

As your Whippet becomes more elderly, he may suffer from arthritis, which you will see as general stiffness, particularly when he gets up after resting. It will help if you ensure his bed is in a warm draft-free location, and if your Whippet gets wet after exercise, you must dry him thoroughly.

If your Whippet seems to be in pain, consult your vet who will be able to help with pain relief medication.

For more information on inherited disorders, see page 182.

Skin problems

If your dog is scratching or nibbling at his skin, first check he is free from fleas (see page 167). There are other external parasites which cause itching and hair loss, but you will need a vet to help you find the culprit.

An allergic reaction, which could be traced to fleas, diet, or environmental factors such as dust mites or pollen, can cause major skin problems. However, it can be quite an undertaking to find the cause of the allergy; you will need to follow your vet's advice, which often requires eliminating specific ingredients from the diet, as well as looking at environmental factors.

See Alopecia, page 184.

Breed-specific disorders

Like all pedigree dogs, the Whippet does have a few breed-related disorders. If diagnosed with any of the diseases listed below, it is important to remember that they can affect offspring, so breeding from affected dogs should be avoided.

There are now recognised screening tests to enable breeders to check for affected individuals and hence reduce the prevalence of these diseases within the breed.

DNA testing is also becoming more widely available, and as research into the different genetic diseases progresses, more DNA tests are being developed.

Alopecia

This refers to hair loss; there are many different causes, which may or may not be hereditary. However, the Whippet is predisposed to the following:

Hyperthyroidism: A condition involving an over-active thyroid gland. Signs of the disease include hair loss.

Colour-dilution alopecia: This affects Whippets with blue or fawn coats, and is first seen as a thinning of hair at around six months. Secondary infections may be treated with antibiotics.

Pattern alopecia: Hair loss occurs in specific areas of the body such as the abdomen, throat and backs of thighs. There is no treatment.

Cushings disease

This is most commonly caused by a tumor in the pituitary gland, which is located near the brain, and more rarely by a tumor in the adrenal glands, which are near the kidneys. Symptoms are various but they mimic the ageing process and can be easy to miss. Treatment with medication substantially improves the affected dog's quality of life.

Eye disorders

Glaucoma

This is when abnormal pressure builds up within the eye. It is caused by a clogging of the drainage system, which removes fluids from the eye. The excessive pressure can cause irreversible damage to the optic nerve, resulting in loss of vision.

Veterinary tests are needed to confirm this condition.

Hereditary cataracts

These may affect one or both eyes. The clouding of the lens may be complete or partial, which will determine how much vision remains. Onset can be as early as six months or as late as seven years of age. Surgery to remove a cataract can be effective, but there is a danger of complications.

The Canine Eye Registration Foundation (CERF), in the US, recommends annual eye testing, and affected dogs should not be bred from.

Progressive retinal atrophy (PRA)

The cells of the retina, which lines the back of the eye, receive light stimuli from the external environment. These 'messages' are transmitted by the brain and interpreted as vision. When a dog is suffering from PRA, the retinal cells deteriorate resulting in blindness, usually affecting both eyes. Early signs are the inability to see in low light conditions.

Sudden Acquired Retinal Degeneration Syndrome (SARDS)

This is a rapid degeneration of the retina leading to complete loss of vision in a few days or weeks. Diagnosis is difficult as the retina appears normal when first examined because the deterioration is so rapid.

Immune mediated disease

This refers to a condition where the body is attacked by its own immune system. It takes various forms depending on what cells are under attack and can result in polyarthritis, anaemia, hyperthyroidism and Addisons disease (malfunctioning of the adrenal gland). Treatment depends on the individual case.

Megaesophagus

This refers to an abnormality of the oesophagus – the tube which transfers food from the mouth to the stomach. In affected dogs, the oesophagus fails to contract, and so instead of food being pushed into the stomach it stays in the oesophagus until it is eventually regurgitated. A dog may also lose the reflex which prevents breathing while food is swallowed, causing food to be inhaled. Treatment is by managing the condition with an appropriate diet, and preventing the dog moving for at least 10 minutes after eating.

Mitral valve disease

Dogs affected by Mitral valve disease (MVD) may not show any functional impairment for many years. Once clinical signs do appear, medication will be required and this is likely to be necessary for the remainder of the dog's life.

Early signs may include increased panting, coughing or tiring easily while on walks, or following over-exertion in hot weather. However, many dogs live for years with heart problems and, while dogs known to be affected should not be used for breeding, such animals can continue to lead happy lives for a long time.

The condition is caused by a physical defect in the mitral valve located in the heart, which results in blood being pumped inefficiently. In severe cases it may cause a build-up of fluid in the chest, resulting in coughing, and collapse, as the muscles are deprived of well-oxygenated blood. Heart medications have greatly improved over the last decade. They are now much safer and can be given for long periods without undue complications

Summing up

It may give the Whippet owner cause for concern to find about health problems that can affect their dog. But it is important to bear in mind that acquiring some basic knowledge is an asset, as it will allow you to spot signs of trouble at an early stage. Early diagnosis is very often the means to the most effective treatment.

Fortunately, the Whippet is generally healthy and disease-free, with his only visits to the vet being annual check-ups. In most cases, owners can look forward to enjoying many happy years with this affectionate and highly entertaining companion.

Useful addresses

Breed & Kennel Clubs
Please contact your Kennel Club to obtain contact information about breed clubs in your area.

UK
The Kennel Club (UK)
1 Clarges Street London, W1J 8AB
Telephone: 0870 606 6750
Fax: 0207 518 1058
Web: www.thekennelclub.org.uk

USA
American Kennel Club (AKC)
5580 Centerview Drive, Raleigh, NC 27606.
Telephone: 919 233 9767
Fax: 919 233 3627
Email: info@akc.org
Web: www.akc.org

United Kennel Club (UKC)
100 E Kilgore Rd, Kalamazoo,
MI 49002-5584, USA.
Tel: 269 343 9020
Fax: 269 343 7037
Web:www.ukcdogs.com/

Australia
Australian National Kennel Council (ANKC)
The Australian National Kennel Council is the administrative body for pure breed canine affairs in Australia. It does not, however, deal directly with dog exhibitors, breeders or judges. For information pertaining to breeders, clubs or shows, please contact the relevant State or Territory Body.

International
Fédération Cynologique Internationalé (FCI)
Place Albert 1er, 13, B-6530 Thuin, Belgium.
Tel: +32 71 59.12.38
Fax: +32 71 59.22.29
Web: www.fci.be/

Training and behavior
UK
Association of Pet Dog Trainers
Telephone: 01285 810811
Web: http://www.apdt.co.uk

Canine Behaviour
Association of Pet Behaviour Counsellors
Telephone: 01386 751151
Web: http://www.apbc.org.uk/

USA
Association of Pet Dog Trainers
Tel: 1 800 738 3647
Web: www.apdt.com/

American College of Veterinary Behaviorists
Web: http://dacvb.org/

American Veterinary Society of Animal Behavior
Web: www.avsabonline.org/

Australia
APDT Australia Inc
Web: www.apdt.com.au

For details of regional behaviorists, contact the relevant State or Territory Controlling Body.

Activities

UK

Agility Club
http://www.agilityclub.co.uk/

British Flyball Association
Telephone: 01628 829623
Web: http://www.flyball.org.uk/

USA

North American Dog Agility Council
Web: www.nadac.com/

North American Flyball Association, Inc.
Tel/Fax: 800 318 6312
Web: www.flyball.org/

Australia

Agility Dog Association of Australia
Tel: 0423 138 914
Web: www.adaa.com.au/

NADAC Australia
Web: www.nadacaustralia.com/

Australian Flyball Association
Tel: 0407 337 939
Web: www.flyball.org.au/

International

World Canine Freestyle Organisation
Tel: (718) 332-8336
Web: www.worldcaninefreestyle.org

Health

UK

British Small Animal Veterinary Association
Tel: 01452 726700
Web: http://www.bsava.com/

Royal College of Veterinary Surgeons
Tel: 0207 222 2001
Web: www.rcvs.org.uk

Alternative Veterinary Medicine Centre
Tel: 01367 710324
Web: www.alternativevet.org/

USA

American Veterinary Medical Association
Tel: 800 248 2862
Web: www.avma.org

American College of Veterinary Surgeons
Tel: 301 916 0200
Toll Free: 877 217 2287
Web: www.acvs.org/

Canine Eye Registration Foundation
The Veterinary Medical DataBases
1717 Philo Rd, PO Box 3007,
Urbana, IL 61803-3007
Tel: 217-693-4800
Fax: 217-693-4801
Web: http://www.vmdb.org/cerf.html

Orthopaedic Foundation of Animals
2300 E Nifong Boulevard
Columbia, Missouri, 65201-3806
Tel: 573 442-0418
Fax: 573 875-5073
Web: http://www.offa.org/

American Holistic Veterinary Medical
Association
Tel: 410 569 0795
Web: www.ahvma.org/

Australia

Australian Small Animal Veterinary
Association
Tel: 02 9431 5090
Web: www.asava.com.au

Australian Veterinary Association
Tel: 02 9431 5000
Web: www.ava.com.au

Australian College Veterinary Scientists
Tel: 07 3423 2016
Web: http://acvsc.org.au

Australian Holistic Vets
Web: www.ahv.com.au/